GOD'S LOVE FOR US

The Story of Jesus' Death and Resurrection
Mark 15:6–16:7 for children

Written by Todd A. Peperkorn

Illustrated by Andre Ceolin

CONCORDIA PUBLISHING HOUSE · SAINT LOUIS

This is the story of our Lord,
Who died and rose again.
His love beyond all thought and dream
Frees us from all our sin.

Our Lord was brought before the crowd.
(The trial they'd forego.)
Barabbas, too, from prison came.
Which one would be let go?

"Should I release Him," Pilate asked,
"This king of all the Jews?"
"No! Crucify!" the crowd replied.
"He's not the one we choose."

So Pilate gave them what they asked,
And guards led Him away.
"King of the Jews, all hail," they said.
(This was on Good Friday.)

Those soldiers mocked and hurt the Lord,
Took off His clothes, and then
They put on Him a crown of thorns
And changed His clothes again.

When they were done, they led Him out
To walk up to the hill,
Out to the place they called "The Skull."
(The prophecy fulfilled.)

And as they went, they grabbed a man
Who also walked the road.
His name was Simon, of Cyrene.
He helped with Jesus' load.

They crucified our Jesus Christ.
His blood for us He shed.
A sign told people who He was;
"King of the Jews," it read.

There were two others there that day,
A robber on each side.
"Come down," they teased, "down from the cross.
And save yourself!" they cried.

They all made fun of Jesus' plight,
E'en though He was in pain.
"You would destroy the temple, ha!"
"Then build it in three days."

INRI

The darkness came, then, on the land.
From noon to three was night.
Then Jesus cried out loud and said,
"My God! You've left Me. Why?"

Then someone there filled up a sponge
With sour wine for Him.
But Jesus didn't take a sip.
And then it was the end.

Lord Jesus breathed His last that day.
Though innocent, He died.
For all the sins of all the world
The Lord was crucified.

The curtain then was torn in two,
And Jesus' work was done.
A soldier then stood up and said,
"This man is God the Son!"

The women who looked on then saw
The place where Jesus lay.
They cared for Him still while He lived,
And now while in the grave.

On Sunday, they went to the tomb
And got a big surprise.
"He lives," the angel said with joy.
"You see—He did arise!"

We give all glory to our God.
We lift our voices high.
The Father, Son, and Holy Ghost
We praise and glorify.

To the Parent:

When we teach our children about Jesus, we tend to focus on the happy stories: that His birth is why we celebrate Christmas, that He welcomed the children to His side, that He healed a little girl who was very ill. To be sure, these events teach how Jesus shows His love for us and are important to learn. But the events of Holy Week that culminate in Good Friday, as difficult as they are to talk about with children, are critical to our understanding of the broad, deep, limitless love Jesus has for us.

Children may wonder why anyone would hurt Jesus, our best friend and helper. They may not understand why the religious leaders and Pilate would send Jesus to the cross. They may question why people made fun of Him. Teaching about Good Friday allows you to explain that everyone sins and that all sin is a betrayal of Jesus. God works through these terrible things to fulfill His plan for our good. Yes, Jesus died and was buried. But then He was alive again, and by this we can be sure that because we believe in Him as our Savior, we will live with Him forever.

As you read this book, ask your child to tell you the story in his or her own words. Discuss the illustrations. And talk specifically about the "good" of Good Friday, which is the great love God has for us in the work and person of Jesus, who took the punishment for all our sins and gives us eternal life.

Pray: We praise You, Jesus! How broad, how deep, how high is Your love for us. Amen.